A Basic Dao

An Introduction to The Way

Compiled by Kuijie Zhou

Translated from the Chinese by

Philip Robyn

LONG RIVER PRESS

San Francisco

Published in the United States of America by
Long River Press
360 Swift Ave., Suite 48
South San Francisco, CA 94080
www.longriverpress.com

Editor: Chris Robyn
Book and cover design: Tommy Liu

First Edition, 2009

ISBN 978-1-59265-077-4

Library of Congress Cataloging-in-Publication Data

Zhou, Kuijie.
A basic Dao : an introduction to the way / compiled by Kuijie Zhou ; translated from the Chinese by Philip Robyn with Xia Weilan.
p. cm.
ISBN 978-1-59265-077-4 (pbk.)
1. Laozi. Dao de jing. 2. Philosophy, Chinese--To 221 B.C. I. Title.
BL1900.L35Z55 2008
299.5'1482--dc22

2008018290

Introduction

Of all the historical figures in the Chinese philosophical canon, perhaps none has made a more significant contribution to Eastern *and* Western understanding of personal spiritual and philosophical growth than Laozi (literally: "Master Lao"). Today, Laozi's works, above all the *Dao De Jing* (Tao Te Ching) serve as a key philosophical and even spiritual bridge for millions of people worldwide: how they choose to lead their lives or look at the world. To read Laozi is not the same as experiencing religious epiphany. Rather, the wisdom of Laozi provides additional introspection through which life's decisions and actions can take on additional resonance and meaning.

Of Laozi's origins little is known: most of what we know remains shrouded in myth and mystery. He was most likely born in the State of Chu during the Zhou Dynasty in the 6th Century B.C. On the one hand, Laozi was known to be a skilled record-keeper and an expert in the rites and affairs of the State. By the same token, he also represents the archetype of the Chinese philosopher/hermit, and was said to have instructed Confucius and even Buddha during his travels. Though Laozi attracted a fair number of followers, he is said to have journeyed in anonimity, preferring to note that, according to the Dao, the place of humans in the world was of little significance.

The legend of the Dao De Jing tells that Laozi, upon journeying far to China's west, at long last reached the furthest frontier post of the empire. By this time his name and reputation were known, and the garrison commanders were on the look-out for "an old man journeying West." Before Laozi passed from the borders of China forever, he was asked to leave a token of his wisdom behind. The result was the Dao De Jing, an approximately 5,000-Chinese character treatise. In the original Chinese, it is a work of prose: it is everything and it is nothing. The Dao De Jing can reveal immense vistas of knowledge and understanding, but how you read and interpret such "revelations," figuratively speaking, is the key to how the text can help you. Thought it is not a long work, it has offered generations of readers new insights on philosophy and thought that can be applicable to those in all walks of life. As with other Chinese philosophers such as Sunzi, Confucius, and Mencius, "Daoist" writings have been used and adapted for derivative works in the field of business, sports, and personal improvement. These classic texts of Chinese philosophy have proven themselves to be as viable today as they were thousands of years ago.

The Dao De Jing gained popularity during the Han Dynasty, as China began to enter a new Golden Age of knowledge and understanding. This peaked during the Tang Dynasty, where Laozi's works became the gospel truth of the Daoist school. The two remain integrally intertwined to this day.

The quotes in this book come from the writings of Laozi. Each is pared with an historical corollary on the opposite page. In this way, the essence of the historical significance of the Dao De Jing is preserved; readers can contemplate how The Dao can be used to influence their lives in today's rapidly-shrinking world. For those involved in philosophy, philanthropy, meditation, self-help, or the understanding of the place of humans in the universe, there is much than can still be gained from such sage words.

A BASIC DAO

During the Five Dynasties (A.D. 907-960) period there was a prime minister named Feng Dao, who had hordes of sycophants and hangers-on around him at all times. One day, one of these individuals was trying to explain the *Dao* but encountered a difficult problem right from the start. In ancient times, it was considered taboo to utter directly the name of any venerated person or thing. The very beginning of the *Dao De Jing* states: "The *Dao* that can be spoken of is not the eternal *Dao*." So, how could this be explained? The '"*Dao*" that could be spoken of' could not actually be uttered, because the character "*Dao*" was part of the name of Feng Dao, and, thus, was not subject to this taboo. But this sycophant, in a flash of inspiration, rendered the phrase "the *Dao* that can be spoken of is not the eternal *Dao*" as "unspeakable...unspeakable... extraordinarily unspeakable." Unwittingly, his belabored circumlocution touched upon the true meaning of "*Dao*" after all, for "*Dao*" in actuality cannot be spoken of, and what is spoken of is no longer "*Dao*".

The *Dao* that can be spoken of is not the eternal *Dao*; the name that can be named is not the eternal name.

道可道非常道
名可名非常名

海粟仁世兄屬題
南海康同璧

A hall full of gold and jade cannot be protected.

Money can buy anything, even misfortune.

In ancient China, there lived a large insect that liked very much to carry things on its back. As it crawled along, whatever object it encountered, it would find a way to carry it on its back, and the farther it went, the heavier grew the load on its back. Without caring whether it could bear the weight or not, it never stopped adding more things to its back, and finally, as the number of things on its back grew greater and greater and the load became heavier and heavier, it was so weighted down that it could no longer crawl. The people who saw it felt very sorry for it, and they took the things off its back. But after a while it got up, and right away proceeded to put more things on its back again. In order to get away from the people, this strange insect crawled with its burden high up into the trees. Though it did its utmost to keep crawling, it instead fell back to the ground and died, crushed under all its hoarded objects. The people observed how the insect's greed brought about its demise.

A knife need only be sharp enough to be useable; if overly sharpened, the cutting edge will break.

Confucius was leading his disciple Zi Gong in paying a visit to the ancestral temple of Duke Huan of the kingdom of Lu. In the temple, he saw a famous water vessel known as "*you e*". Confucius told Zi Gong to fetch some water and pour it in. When the vessel was half full, it stood perfectly upright, but when it was completely full, the vessel suddenly tipped over. In an epiphany, he exclaimed to his disciple, "So! This must be what 'having a surfeit' means!" Zi Gong asked, "Master, how can it be kept full without tipping over?"

"By controlling and diminishing the water." Replied Confucius.

Zi Gong then asked, "What is 'possessing a surfeit'?"

Confucius explained: “The myriad things are born and grow, and when they reach their maximum they begin to tend toward decline. For instance, when the sun reaches noon, it then tends toward the west and begins to set behind the mountains; on the fifteenth day of the month, the moon is round and full, but then the waxing moon begins to wane. Man is also like this. When he has reached utmost joy, he will move toward sorrow. For this reason, the intelligent man must conserve with stupidity; the valiant and stalwart man must conserve with timidity and cowardice; those with extensive knowledge must conserve with parochial ignorance; and the wealthy and privileged must conserve with modesty and caution.”

The twisted or tortuous can be preserved; the bent can be straightened; the sagging or depleted can be made plentiful; the old can be reborn as new; those who take little will obtain much, while those who are covetous will be perplexed.

An aspiring diplomat named Tian Jiu once sought an audience with King Hui of Qin, but unfortunately he waited in the kingdom of Qin for three years without being able to meet the king.

Then someone recommended Tian Jiu to the King of Chu, so Tian Jiu went from the kingdom of Qin to the kingdom of Chu and paid a formal visit to the King of Chu, who greatly appreciated Tian Jiu and sent him as a diplomatic envoy to the kingdom of Qin, where he finally met King Hui.

Upon exiting from his audience with King Hui, Tian Jiu let out a long sigh, and said to his entourage, "I remained in the Kingdom of Qin for three years without meeting King Hui, never thinking that the road to meeting the monarch of Qin actually lay in the kingdom of Chu."

Thus the way in which a man of insight handles affairs need not resemble a rope pulled taut, following only a straight path; rather, one must not hesitate to follow a roundabout way in order to achieve one's goal.

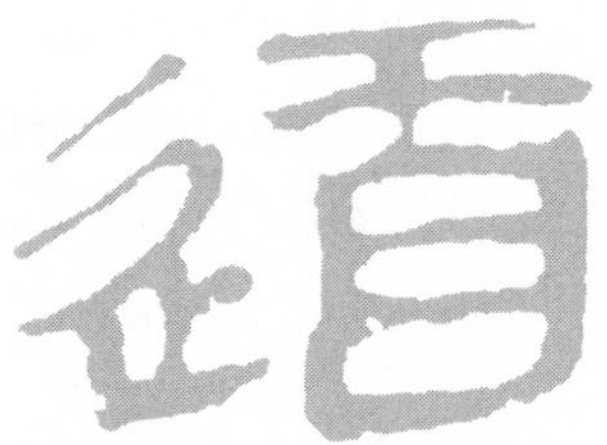

The Master Does Not Strive; Thus None Under Heaven Can Strive With Him.

A middle-aged man had a happy family and success in his undertakings, yet he nevertheless felt very dejected. A physician prescribed four remedies for him, placing them into four small medicine pouches and advising him to go alone a day hence to the seashore, open the medicine pouches and take the remedies individually at four equal intervals until the sun set. The middle-aged man trusted him but remained somewhat skeptical.

The next day, he arrived at the seashore, and at once he opened the first remedy pouch, but all there was was a slip of paper on which was written "listen." So with rapt attention he listened to the sound of the waves striking the shore, the sounds of seabirds calling, the sound of the sea breeze – these sounds of Nature brought him tranquility, and he suddenly realized that he had not listened with such concentration like that for a considerably long time.

The second remedy pouch had only a piece of paper written, "recollect." The middle-aged man recalled the vicissitudes of earlier years when he was establishing himself, the ups and downs of those times. Remembering with gratitude many persons and events, he couldn't help breaking into a smile.

The third remedy pouch held a slip of paper on which was written "examine motivation." He began to ask himself: what was the purpose of pursuing libations and sensual pleasure like a slave? What kind of life did he really want after all?

The last remedy pouch contained a slip of paper saying "write your worries in the sand." He picked up a stick and on the sand wrote all his worries, his pressures, his sources of dejection. He stood beside the words deep in thought, and as the tide came in, all his worries "worries" were washed away without a trace by the water. At twilight, the middle-aged man returned home with a happy and carefree heart.

Weakness Overcomes Strength.

Sun Bin and Pang Juan were both students of Gui Gu Zi, the "Master of Demon Valley". For their graduation examination, the Master presented this topic: Gui Gu Zi is sitting in a room, and the students must find a way to make him leave the room; whoever succeeds passes the test.

Pang Juan went first. He used the beautiful scenery outside to entice the Master out to enjoy it, but Gui Gu Zi was unmoved. Then Pang Juan was going to start a fire to burn the house down. Gui Gu Zi said, "This will never do. Before you can light the fire, I shall appear and stop it." Pang Juan did not pass the examination, and slowly withdrew from the examination hall.

Upon arriving at the examination hall, Sun Bin expressed that such a test was unfair to Pang Juan, because Pang had gone first, and Sun, going afterwards, could benefit from Pang's experience. In order to ensure a fair test, the topic should be changed. Will Master please go out of the room and let me find a way to have Master enter the room? Feeling that this was reasonable, Gui Gu Zi indicated, "Fine! I'll go outside and let you cause me to come in; isn't it the same thing?"

As soon as Gui Gu Zi went outside, Sun Bin said mirthfully, "Master, I have resolved the topic you presented: I got you to go out of the room."

Use the World to Look at the World.

Zhuang Zi was visiting the Chestnut Garden, when he suddenly saw flying from the south a large, strange bird. Its wingspan was seven feet across, and it had enormous eyes. It bumped against Zhuang Zi's forehead before coming to rest in a tree. Zhuang Zi found this most strange, and thought: what bird is this? It has such big wings, yet it cannot fly far; such big eyes, yet it cannot see clearly. So he picked up a stone and quietly approached. Suddenly, he also saw a cicada resting on a small branch, and next to the cicada was a praying mantis with forelegs raised, about to seize it. The praying mantis was so intent on its prey that it forgot its own body was exposed, and the strange bird was just about to eat the praying mantis.

Just then, Zhuang Zi suddenly came to the realization that when a man sees gain he forgets about harm, and so he dropped the stone and fled. When the caretaker of the Chestnut Garden saw someone running, he thought it was someone stealing chestnuts, and he pursued Zhuang Zi, cursing loudly.

When Zhuang Zi got back home he felt uneasy, and he didn't set foot outside for three days. His student Lin Qie asked, "Master, why have you been unhappy these past few days?" Zhuang Zi said, "I have been strictly paying attention to the extrinsic nature of things, but I have ignored their intrinsic nature. When I see muddy water, I remain oblivious of the clear pool. When I was walking in the Chestnut Garden, startled to see a strange bird skimming past, I forgot myself, and I suffered the scolding of the gardener. This is why I have been feeling unhappy."

This tale tells us that in observing problems there are

different starting points and different points of focus or emphasis, consequently leading to different conclusions.

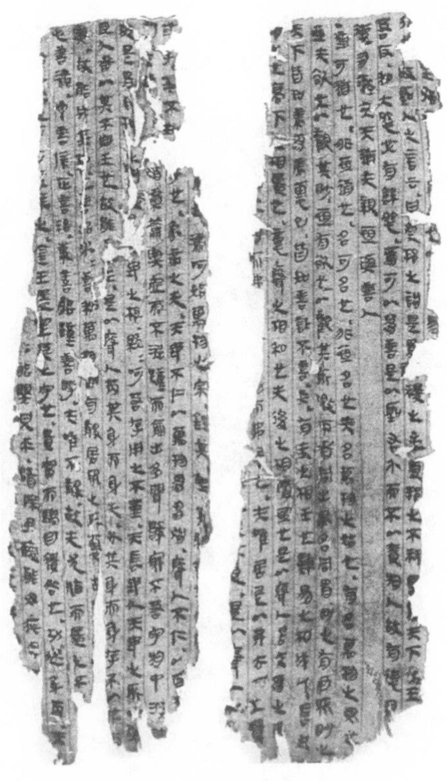

On misfortune perches happiness; beneath happiness lurks misfortune.

Near a frontier fortress there was an old man, whom people called "Sai Weng" (Old Man of the Forest). For reasons unknown, his horse disappeared into the land of the barbarians, and everyone came to console him. Sai Weng, however, said, "How do we know that this is not a fortunate thing?" After a few months, his lost horse came back leading a fine steed from the barbarian lands, and everyone came to congratulate him. He said, "How do we know this is not a misfortune?" Sai Weng's son loved to ride horses, but one time he fell from the horse and broke his thigh, and everyone came to see how he was. Sai Weng said, "How do we know that this is not a fortunate thing?" A year later, the barbarians launched a major invasion against the frontier fortress, and all the able-bodied men were sent to fight; nine out of ten were killed in battle, leaving only the son, whose broken leg had exempted him from being drafted into the ranks. Father and son remained safe.

Difficult tasks must be done by starting with an easy aspect; great tasks must be done by breaking them into small tasks.

King Zhou was a tyrant of the Shang Dynasty. When he first came to power, the entire court of civilian and military officials thought that the power of the kingdom would be as steadfast as a boulder; only Jizi, the king's uncle, remained in low spirits.

One day, King Zhou ordered someone to make a pair of ivory chopsticks, and when Jizi saw them, he was beside himself with dread. Nobody else was able to understand this, and they all said he was needlessly worried over troubles of his own imagining. Jizi said, "Once the monarch uses ivory chopsticks, he will no longer use an ordinary earthen bowl to hold his rice. He will change to use a rhinoceros horn as a cup and a bowl made of beautiful jade as a rice bowl. Once he has ivory chopsticks, a rhinoceros horn cup, and a jade bowl, do you think he will still want cheap tea and ordinary food? His dining table will have to be heaped with delicacies. And he will no longer be willing to wear clothes of rough homespun cloth; rather, he will wear only the finest silks. He will no longer want to live in a humble thatched cottage but rather a sumptuous palace, and he will build tall towers and pavilions for his enjoyment. Where will all of this lead? So when I saw the sovereign using the ivory chopsticks, I shuddered at the unbearable, unimaginable consequences." As one might have expected, because of King Zhou's extravagance, the Shang Dynasty was destroyed by the Zhou Dynasty less than five years later.

Without doing, there can be no failure; without grasping, no loss.

Emperor Qianlong of the Qing Dynasty went south on an imperial procession to the Gold Mountain Temple at Zhenjiang, and stood on the top of a mountain, accompanied by the honorable abbot Fa Qing, to enjoy the view of the Yangtze River. Qianlong asked the monk Fa Qing: "How many boats pass by on the river each day?" The monk said, "There are only two boats." Qianlong found this strange: "Why are there only two boats?" The monk Fa Qing said, "One is for fame, and one is for profit; thus, there are only two boats."

Men who chase after fame and profit have only two emotions: the joy of gain and the sorrow of loss.

A peaceful situation is easy to manage; the unportentous is easy to plan for; the brittle is easy to sunder; and the minute is easy to scatter.

The famous physician, known as Bian Que, went to pay his respects to Duke Huan of Cai. After a while, he said to the Duke, "Your Highness has an illness, but it's only in the surface layer of the skin beneath your eye. If this does not receive timely treatment, I fear that it will worsen."

Duke Huan of Cai was nonchalant. "I'm fine. I don't have any illness at all." After Bian Que departed, Duke Huan of Cai said, "Doctors always like to say that healthy people are sick, as an excuse to vaunt their medical brilliance."

Ten days later, Bian Que came once again to pay his respects to Duke Huan of Cai, and once again he reminded him, "Your Highness's illness has already spread into the muscle; if it is not treated right away, it will grow more and more serious." When he heard this, Duke Huan grew quite annoyed, and he paid no heed whatsoever to Bian Que's sincere advice.

After another ten days had passed, Bian Que came once again. He said, "Your Highness's illness has already spread to the gastrointestinal tract. If it is not treated, it will get worse." Duke Huan still paid him no heed, and he was even more annoyed.

When yet another ten days had passed, Bian Que turned and fled at the mere sight of Duke Huan. Duke Huan dispatched someone to chase him and find out what the matter was. Bian Que answered, "When the illness was in the surface of the skin, it could have been cured by a hot compress of a medicinal decoction; when it was in the muscles, it could have been cured by acupuncture and moxibustion; when it was in the gastrointestinal tract, it could have been cured by a clear, hot medicinal decoction to relieve inflammation. But once the illness is in the bones, only Heaven knows what will happen. Now Your Highness's illness has entered the bones, and there is nothing more that I can do."

After another five days, Duke Huan of Cai ached all over, and he sent someone to look for Bian Que; but Bian Que had already departed for the Kingdom of Qin. Duke Huan of Cai died soon thereafter.

A tree of great girth grows from a tiny sprout; a nine-story platform is based upon piled-up earth; a thousand-mile journey begins beneath one's feet.

At the end of the Eastern Han Dynasty, there was a man of letters called Chen Fan. He was disturbed by the sight of widespread warfare and the oppression of the populace, and he therefore made up his mind to rectify the situation. His fellow villagers had high expectations of him, and he also thought very highly of himself. Accordingly, he shirked trivial matters, disdaining involvement in trifles, to the point that his house was filled with cobwebs, dirty, and in great disarray.

Having heard of his great reputation, a scholar came to pay his respects, but upon entering his house and seeing the chaotic mess, he was taken aback, and asked, "Master, why do you not clean up your house?"

Chen Fan said indignantly, “The great man should clean up the world on behalf of the kingdom, not sweep out his own house.”

But the scholar said in disapproval, “You cannot even clean up an area as small as your hand; how can you possibly clean up the world?”

When the Great Dao was cast aside, there came benevolence and righteousness.

The Han Dynasty governed the world by means of filial piety; there was a system for raising the filial and upright to hold official position.

At that time, there was a man known as Xu Wu who was promoted due to his filial piety, but his two younger brothers were unable to find an opportunity to make their way in the world. One day, Xu Wu expressed to his two younger brothers the need to divide the household. He divided their property into three portions, taking the fertile fields, grand residence, and able-bodied servants for himself and leaving but very little for the two brothers. But they made no complaint to their older brother.

After this happened, the villagers all praised Xu Wu's brothers for their complaisance and decorum, the epitome of love and respect for their elder brother; and they rebuked Xu Wu for his avarice. Because of all this, the two younger brothers also received official appointments. But Xu Wu, who remained unhappy over the whole thing, convened his clansmen and told them that he had done this solely to give his two younger brothers a leg up, and that now he was going to return the property and three times the profits to them. When this became widely known, Xu Wu received a promotion of three grades, to the position of minor prefect.

The Master has no mind of his own; his mind is the mind of the People.

During the Tang Dynasty there was a man called Han Xiu who was a palace official. Whenever the emperor said or did something slightly inappropriate, Han Xiu would submit memorials remonstrating him, thus often putting the emperor, Tang Xuan Zong (Li Long Ji), in an awkward situation.

Whenever Tang Xuan Zong was feasting in the palace or hunting in the game preserve and something went the slightest bit awry, he would ask his followers, "Does Han Xiu know about this?" Right after these words were said, a scolding memorial from Han Xiu would arrive. The emperor was often greatly discomfited by this.

One day, Tang Xuan Zong was looking at himself in

the mirror, and said with a sigh, "I've gotten a lot thinner recently." The eunuch next to him immediately said, "Since Han Xiu has become a minister, Your Majesty has grown even thinner than in the past; why not drive him away?"

Tang Xuan Zong sighed in admiration, "Although I may look thin, the nation must be fat. I employ Han Xiu for the benefit of the nation, not for myself."

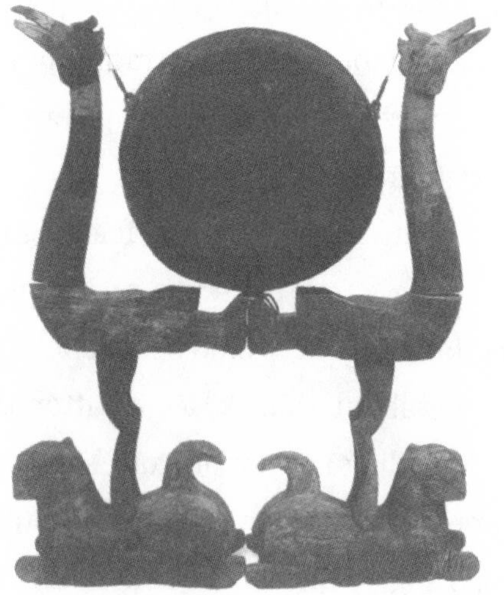

The one who knows does not speak, the one who speaks does not know.

A man went to a bird shop and there saw two parakeets. First he looked at one of them, and when he found that the bird could imitate human speech, he asked the shopkeeper, “How much is this one?” The shopkeeper replied that it was a hundred dollars. Then he tried the other one, only to discover that the second bird was incapable of imitating human speech. Again he asked the shopkeeper, “How much for this one?” The shopkeeper replied, five hundred dollars. The man thought this quite strange, and he asked, “Why does the one that speaks cost only a hundred dollars and the one that doesn’t speak cost five hundred?” The shopkeeper replied, “Well, even though that one cannot speak, he can ponder!"

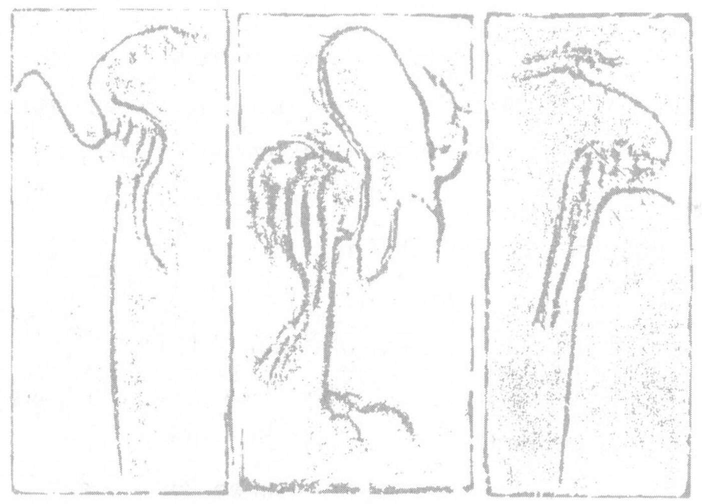

Though two neighboring states are so near to one another that they can each hear the sounds of the other's chickens and dogs, yet their people grow old and die without knowing one another.

During the Tai-Yuan period (376-396) of the Jin dynasty, a fisherman of Wu-ling boated along a stream. Heedless of how far he had gone, he suddenly saw a grove of peach trees. For several hundred paces it was all peach trees. At the source of the stream in the peach grove he saw a mountain, and after entering an opening in the mountain and walking several paces it suddenly opened out into a broad plain whereupon there lay neatly-built houses and crisscrossing roads. The sounds of chickens and dogs could be heard, and the men and women went about their farming tasks, while the elderly and the young were contented and happy. The people of the

Peach Spring were greatly astonished to see the fisherman, whom they invited to their homes as a guest, saying that their ancestors had come to that place to avoid the chaos of war at the time of the Qin Dynasty. They were cut off from the world and had no knowledge whatsoever of the Han Dynasty or the Wei and Jin dynasties. The fisherman stayed there for several days before returning home. The Peach Blossom Spring as depicted by Tao Yuan Ming epitomizes the political ideals of Laozi and Zhuangzi.

If the worthy are not advanced, then the people will not strive; if hard-to-obtain products are not held in esteem, then the people will not steal; if they do not see covetous things, then the people's hearts will not be confused.

Wang An Shi of the Song Dynasty (960-1279) advocated political reforms, implementing the 'green shoots law' and the 'equal transport law', and so on. He also ordered that the peasants of the various administrative prefectures be compelled to store fertilizer.

There was a city official who implemented this in an especially severe manner, compelling each group of households to hand over 5,000 kilos of night soil within a set time period lest they be fined one hundred ounces of silver. The leader of the group of households hounded them day and night, and on the last day of the set period the peasants could only scrape together 4,950 kilograms; they were 50 kilograms (one dan) short. The peasants, having no alternative, pooled their resources and bought several hundred catties of red amaranth, which they boiled until done, squeezed out the red liquid, and offered as night soil so as to have enough to turn over to the officials.

The sharp-eyed petty official who received the night soil said, "Why is this dan [50 kilos] of night soil dripping such red liquid?" The leader of the group of households hemmed and hawed, and broke out in a cold sweat. Finally he turned and said indignantly, "Hey, old man, how about giving us a break? We've been saving fertilizer for a whole year, and not only did we not harvest much grain, but you've even squeezed all the shit out of the peasants' bellies. So take this bloody stool or not, as you please!"

Wang An Shi was a worthy and talented man who strove for political reform. In order to win support, he did not hesitate to make friendly alliances with bad men, which resulted in his being exploited by these bad men, creating severe problems for society.

When acting without contravening nature, there is nothing that cannot be managed.

Just after Emperor Wen of Han ascended the throne, he issued an imperial edict to abolish the law whereby the families of criminals were also imprisoned, thus winning the hearts of the people. Next he issued another imperial edict to render assistance to widowers, widows, orphans, and seniors without children, as well as the destitute. He knew well that with one careless move, there were those who would seek advantage and that an unhealthy climate would result. Therefore, he issued an edict of 'no receipt of tribute', ordering all quarters that they need not offer tribute.

Time after time, Emperor Wen of Han reduced or

remitted taxation and encouraged the peasants' 'honest labor'; in addition, he himself was thrifty and frugal, and during his 23 years on the throne there was no increase of palatial dwellings, gardens and parks, dress, and expensive jewelry.

As Emperor Wen of Han thus quietly engaged in non-action, he achieved the goal of not disturbing or harming the people, and as a consequence, the power of the kingdom greatly increased, and the populace lived and worked in peace and contentment, thus creating the new phase of the golden age of Wen and Jing (his son, who succeeded him as emperor).

The noble regards himself as the world, and thus can be trusted with the world.

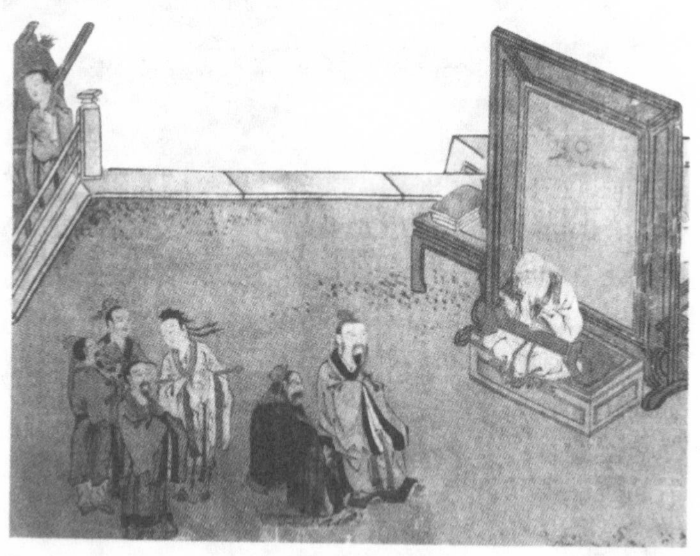

The Great King of Zhou resided at a place called Bin. The barbarians of the north came to attack them, and the Great King offered them tribute of furs, money, and silks, which the barbarians did not accept. He offered tribute of pearls and precious jade, but still the barbarians would not accept it. What the barbarians wanted was land. This being the situation, the Great King said to his people, "Now the foreigners are invading us, and in order that everyone might live and work in peace, I have given them a great deal of property, but they have not stopped their invasion, because their goal is land. I had hoped that on our land we could all live quiet and settled lives. But now, because I have this land, the barbarians are attacking incessantly; and by using this land I have in fact harmed everyone by causing them to suffer the bitterness of war.... Oh, I cannot bear this! In order not to involve you, I shall leave this place."

The Great King trekked across the Liang Mountains and settled below Mt. Qi in Shaanxi Province, but the populace of Bin considered the Great King a good leader, and so they followed him to live below Mt. Qi, opening up a new domain, and this new revitalization eventually consolidated the Great King's base.

Know and accept the norm, such acceptance is fair.

In the fall of the year 200, Yuan Shao led a large army of 100,000 in an attack on Guan Du. At the time, Cao Cao's forces were few, and he was greatly overmatched by Yuan Shao. From the beginning of August until the end of September, Cao Cao's forces were gradually worn out, provisions were inadequate, and all the generals of the central Shaanxi plain maintained neutrality and looked on from the sidelines. His troops were alarmed and uneasy, and many of them made secret alliances with Yuan Shao in order to maintain a bit of room for maneuvering. Then Xu You, one of Yuan Shao's advisers, went over to Cao Cao, who employed his stratagem, burning Yuan

Shao's provisions at Wu Chao and thus allowing victory of the few over the many, and from that time on bringing about an abrupt change in the battle situation.

After the battle of Guan Du was over and the battlefield was being cleared, Cao Cao discovered among Yuan Shao's papers the letters of surrender that those in his camp had secretly written to Yuan Shao. It was suggested to Cao Cao that these men be severely punished, but Cao Cao said, "When Yuan Shao was formidable, even I feared for my life, let alone those men under me." He then ordered that the secret letters be set to the torch and categorically refused to further investigate the matter, thus calming the hearts of his soldiers.

Cao Cao's great forgiveness coincides with Laozi's principle of 'knowing and accepting the norm, such acceptance is fair', and is the main reason he was able to become the mighty hero of his era.

老子

道可道非常道名可名非常名無名天地之始
有名萬物之母常無欲以觀其妙常有欲以觀
其徼此兩者同出而異名同謂之玄玄之又玄衆
妙之門

天下皆知美之為美斯惡已皆知善之為善斯不
善已故有無之相生難易之相成長短之相形高

The best leaders are those whose existence is not known.

A Ming Dynasty Confucianist thus depicted leadership style: generous and deep, far-knowing and widely attentive, benefiting through invisibility, eliminating misfortune through denial, without brilliance or courageous merit, yet the world secretly receives his gifts. Because the people of the world are all shielded by him, so the style of the leader is that it is not really known whether he exists or not. This is exceptionally close to the ideal of Laozi.

When the leader's faith is not enough, there will be faithlessness.

During the Warring States period, Shang Yang prepared regulations for political reform for Duke Xiao of Qin but did not announce them, fearing that the populace did not believe that he would act in accordance with the law. So he erected a thirty-foot-tall wooden post at the southern gate of the capital city of the Kingdom of Qin, and announced that whosoever could move the wooden post to the northern gate of the city would be rewarded with ten pieces of gold. The people considered this very strange, not believing that such a great reward would be given, and nobody went to move the pole. Shang Yang then commanded that the reward be increased to fifty pieces of gold.

So finally someone moved the wooden pole to the northern gate, and Shang Yang bestowed the reward as promised in order to demonstrate that his word could be trusted. Only after winning the trust of the people did Shang Yang implement the regulations for political reform.

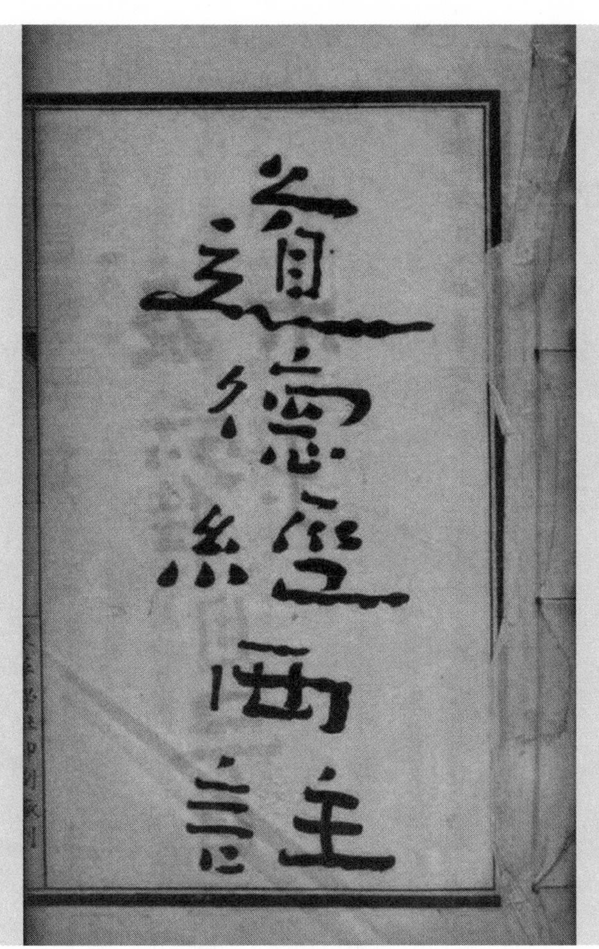
道德經西註

The man who kills cannot succeed in the world.

In the year 1252, Liu Bing Zhong went with Kublai Khan on an expedition against the kingdom of Da Li. Liu was extraordinarily talented and thus appreciated by Kublai, and his views were thus often accepted. He advised Kublai to 'avoid killing' so that the Mongol armies might travel more rapidly.

At the time, the government of the kingdom of Da Li was corrupt; it was a kingdom whose power was on the wane. As Kublai's soldiers neared the city, they first dispatched an envoy to enter the city and call for surrender. Unexpectedly, the kingdom of Da Li refused to surrender; moreover, they beheaded the envoy. Kublai was furious, and ordered that the city be massacred. Liu Bing Zhong remonstrated in protest, saying: "The killing of the envoy was done by the authorities, but the ordinary citizens are blameless." Kublai rescinded the order he had issued, and Liu Bing Zhong proclaimed that killing was to be prohibited, thus preserving the lives and property of the people of Da Li, not one of whom was ungrateful.

A year later, the kingdom of Da Li crumbled.

With the beginning of governance there were titles.

A man named Han Zhao Hou fell into a drunken slumber, and his servant in charge of hats feared he would catch a chill, so he covered him with a garment. When Han Zhao Hou awoke, he was very happy, and asked his attendant, "Who was it who covered me with a garment?" The attendant replied, "The servant in charge of hats covered you." Zhao Hou's expression changed drastically, and he punished both the servant in charge of hats and the servant in charge of clothing. He punished the latter because he had been derelict in his duty, and the former for exceeding his duty.

Seeing that the servant in charge of hats was recalcitrant, he said, “I’m not afraid of catching a chill; what I fear is the worse misfortune that will arise from someone exceeding his duty.” Han Zhao Hou reprimanded his servants that ‘if they weren’t in the other’s position they shouldn’t do the other’s duties’ and pointed out the importance of ‘title’ and ‘function’.

得其所欲故大者宜為下
道者萬物之奧善人之寶不善人之所保美言
可以市尊行可以加人人之不善何棄之有故
立天子置三公雖有拱璧以先駟馬不如坐進
此道古之所以貴此道者何也不曰求以得有
罪以免耶故為天下貴
為無為事無事味無味大小多少報怨以德
圖難於其易為大於其細天下之難事必
作於易天下之大事必作於細是以聖人終不
為大故能成其大夫輕諾必寡信多易多
難是以聖人由難之故終無難矣
其安易持其未兆易謀其脆易泮其微易
散為之於未有治之於未亂合抱之木生於
毫末九層之臺起於累土千里之行始於足
下為者敗之執者失之是以聖人無為故無敗

If you grasp the Great Form, the world will approach.

Duke Ai of Lu said to Confucius, “I have heard a story that there was a man who moved his residence, but he even forgot his wife. Have you ever heard of anyone so absent-minded?”

Confucius sternly replied, “That’s not absent-minded. There once was someone who even forgot their own body!”

Duke Ai of Lu asked in astonishment, “How could that be? Please tell me!”

“The King of the Xia Dynasty was wealthy beyond belief, but he totally forgot the rules and codes of his ancestors, drinking and carousing day and night with seductresses and paying no heed to government; he heeded the fomentations of villains and caused loyal and devoted ministers to flee or remain silent, leading to the collapse of the kingdom. Isn't this an example of forgetting one's own life?"

The fish cannot leave the deep pool, and the sharp weapons of the state cannot be displayed.

One day, Confucius was discussing government with his students, and he asked Zi Xia, "If you were the ruler of a country, how would you carry out your governmental decrees?" Zi Xia deeply pondered the question for a while, and then said, "Ordinarily, I only know phrases and clichés, chanting about the wind and extolling the moon; what do I know of politics?"

Confucius had Zi Xia address the question from a literary point of view.

Zi Xia said, "One day I was strolling on a riverbank, reciting poetry, and I saw a fisherman angling: tail upon silver scaled tail came out of the green water, fell into the dust, flopped around a bit, and then no longer moved; the ripples in the water gradually diminished, and the pool was clear and still as before–it was as though nothing had happened. Thus I came to the realization of a truth: once it has left the water, a fish dies not long afterward; but when the water leaves the fish, it is still water, just as before, and is not affected whatsoever."

Confucius clapped in appreciation, and said, "You have already understood the principles of how to govern."

If the sovereign does not depart from the 'Dao' in managing the kingdom, the water can still be water; however, the tactics that the sovereign employs to unify his ministers he must keep deeply hidden and not divulge, just as the fish cannot leave the water.

In the world, the sage is humble; for the world, he makes his heart simple and unsophisticated. The people heed him well, and the sage treats all as his children.

Duke Mu of Qin set out in a chariot, but the chariot broke down and the horse pulling the chariot ran away and got lost, only to be captured by the locals. Duke Mu of Qin went looking for the horse himself, and on his search he came to the bottom of Mt. Qi, where he discovered that the locals had already killed the horse and were even then jawing upon huge chunks of it.

When Duke Mu of Qin saw this, he sighed and said, "If you eat the flesh of a fine horse without drinking a little wine, you will harm your bodies; what concerns me most is that your bodies will be harmed." Whereupon he called for his subordinates to prepare wine, and had them drink some wine before departing.

The next year, Duke Mu of Qin fought a great battle at Han Yuan against Duke Hui of Jin. The Jin forces were about to surround the chariot of Duke Mu, and Liang You Mi, a senior official of the kingdom of Jin, had blocked Duke Mu's imperial bodyguard. It appeared as though Duke Mu was about to be captured, but just at that moment, about three hundred of the men who had formerly eaten horsemeat at the base of Mt. Qi swarmed forth, giving their all to protect Duke Mu. In the end, there was a great victory over the Jin forces, and Duke Hui of Jin was the one who was captured.

Rule a large kingdom as though you are cooking small fish.

Cui Qu sought the advice of Laozi, saying, "If one does not govern the world, how can people's hearts be directed toward goodness?"

Laozi replied, "By taking care to avoid disturbing people's feelings. When people's hearts are oppressed, they become dejected; when they are inspired, they soar. When feelings and aspirations are dejected or exalted, it is as though people in one minute went up to heaven and in the next minute down to hell. Feelings and aspirations can be soft and yielding, and they can be firm and obdurate. When a person encounters a setback, he may be irascible like a raging inferno or frozen in icy terror. When people's hearts are settled and at peace, their feelings run still and deep; when people's hearts are agitated, they leap and soar upward. People's feelings can be the most obstinate and the most difficult to deal with.

In governing a large nation, things must remain calm and unperturbed, just like fetching water from a well, where you don't want to agitate the water at the well mouth, for the more agitated it becomes, the more the dead leaves and sediment are stirred up and the more turbid the water becomes. Only when it is not perturbed can the well water be clear and pure; only without upheaval can society remain tranquil."

Weapons are inauspicious tools and contemptible objects and thus avoided by those who have the 'Dao'.

In the Kingdom of Qi, ever since Duke Xuan came to power, the kingdom's might increased day by day, and the frequent opening of new territory, engaging in wanton wars of aggression, and rampant murder, the people suffered bitterly.

One day, the philosopher Mo Tzu went to see the King of Qi with the intention of motivating him through words.

Mo Tzu said, "Now here we have a sword that we can use to chop off a man's head. One 'chop', so clean and simple, and the body and head are apart. So is the edge of this sword considered sharp or not?"

The King of Qi said, "Very sharp!"

Mo Tzu then asked, "If we chop off many heads in succession, equally clean and simple, is it considered sharp or not?"

The King of Qi said, "Even sharper!"

So Mo Tzu asked further, "The sword is very sharp; so who will suffer the adversity?"

The King of Qi said, "Of course it is the men who have been decapitated."

Mo Tzu said, "Outward aggression, the annexing of kingdoms and the defeating of armies, and causing armor-wearing and weapon-bearing warriors to leave their bleached bones in far-off lands.... To meet the needs of aggression, excessive taxes are levied at home, expropriating the people's wealth and leaving the elders destitute, filled with anxiety and in desperate straits.... Who will suffer the adversity?"

The King of Qi hung his head, and at long last quietly said, "I will suffer the adversity."

光緒辛卯夏四月上浣山陰任伯年

Empty the mind, maintain tranquility.

A group of people once lived in a valley at the base of the mountain. They were often surrounded by accumulated water on all sides; mosquitoes and flies were abundant, as were infectious diseases, and the people's lives were unspeakably bitter, yet they couldn't think of a good way to improve their environment.

Later, a wise man passed by that place, and the people poured out their woes to him and asked him to tell them how they might improve their environment. The wise man advised them to move up onto the mountain to live, saying that those who lived in valleys were "common men, whereas those who lived on mountains were "immortals". This was the fundamental difference between high and low. Thenceforth the people moved to the mountains and lived on a mountain, leading the happy, fulfilled lives of "immortals" who strove not with the world.

Knowing glory and honor yet maintaining humility.

During the reign of Huangyou of the Song dynasty (1049-1053), the emperor, Song Renzong, sent a eunuch with imperial edict to find Ju Na, a reclusive Buddhist monk, and instructed him to preside at the Xiaoci Temple. But Ju Na refused, claiming that he was ill, and recommended another master, Huai Lian, to accept the emperor's edict.

The eunuch was aghast, "But it's the emperor!" He exclaimed. "How can you not accept?"

Master Ju Na replied, "I am just a humble monk, one of many. My eyesight and hearing are not very good. I am satisfied with my life here in the mountains, drinking water from the spring, and eating vegetables. Even if were to become as enlightened as the Buddha, I would not wish for such gains. What of the rest? It does not concern me. A high reputation is hard to earn."

Avoiding danger by knowing when to stop.

There once was an ambitious young man who wanted to travel abroad to seek his fortune. He purchased a boat and a load of goods he intended to take and sell overseas. Unexpectedly, just a few days after setting sail, a violent storm came and capsized the boat. The boat and all the cargo sank beneath the waves. The young man grabbed onto a piece of wreckage and was borne by the sea to a deserted island. Sitting on the beach, he burst into tears.

Suddenly, a group of island natives surrounded him and exclaimed, "God has granted us a new king!" The young man was puzzled. A wizened old man came close to him. "This is our law," he explained.

"A new king is crowned every year, and he is the first outsider who comes to the island. If you are satisfied with the law, then you shall be the new king. During the period of your reign, you can enjoy great felicity. But do not forget that the throne is only for one year; this time next year you shall lose your crown and will be sent away to that island over there." He pointed across the water to a small, isolated, neighboring island. "If you resist, you shall be killed. This is the law."

Thus, the young man became king of the island. The very next day, he told the natives to go to the small neighboring island and build a house, plant vegetables and fruit trees. The young man enjoyed his rule as king, and, one year later, his crown was removed and he was sent off in a canoe with a paddle to the small island. Because he had prepared for this moment a year ago, he created a haven of peace and happiness for the rest of life.

He who is contented has riches.

There was once a fabulously wealthy man who was keen on making money and accumulating wealth, but worked his servants hard.

One of the wealthy man's servants was an old man, who was ordered around all throughout the day, and at night he fell asleep the moment his head touched the pillow. Every night, the servant dreamed that he was the one to live in luxurious palaces and eat delicious food. Although he had to work as a servant each day, he nevertheless was able to comfort himself: "In a hundred years of life, day and night are each one half. Though I am hard pressed as a servant in the day, I am happy as a king at night! What can I complain about?"

By and by, the wealthy man worried about his property and all his money. At night he often dreamed that he had the seemingly carefree life of a man with no material possessions. Sometimes he even dreamed that he had switched places with the old man servant. One day, the wealthy man fell ill. He told his worries to a friend, and the friend advised him, "You are a man of honor and have a wealthy family. You are far better off than most people. You say you have dreamt that you were rather a servant? Life is full of sweetness and bitterness. Perhaps part of the truth lies in your dream?"

Suddenly, the wealthy man's attitude changed greatly. He treated his servants well, no longer single-mindedly seeking to pursue wealth. Since that time, he felt pleasant and free of pain.

Who understands Others is learned; Who understands the Self is enlightened.

A man named Lao Wang often bought fruit for his family, but he never selected the fruit himself. Instead, he asked the shopkeeper to help him, and the fruits he bought each time were of the best quality.

A friend once asked him, "How are you such an expert at selecting fruit?" Lao Wang said, "Actually, I am not good at selecting fruit, but I am good at selecting a shopkeeper. I find him honest, skilled, and believe he can select better fruits than I can."

Foresight and Virtue are flowers of the Tao.

During the Western Jin Dynasty (AD 265-317), the kingdoms were fighting each other endlessly. At that time, Zhang Han, an aide of King Qi, lived in Luoyang. One year in autumn, with the West Wind blowing, he could not help yearn for the sugar cane soup of his hometown in Wu County. He said, "A happy life is the most precious thing, and how can I be an official thousands of miles away, pursuing reputation and status?" With that, he asked for a small retinue to return to his hometown. Soon, however, King Qi suffered defeat, and his aides were captured or killed. Zhang Han, however, was able to escape. At that time, people thought that Zhang Han had the gift of prophecy, being able to foresee events before they happened. Actually, the reason why he was able to escape the fall of King Qi was that he would rather live a simple life. Not living for or seeking fame and fortune, he did not boast of himself and was able to escape the bureaucratic purge of the other Qi aides.

There is no greater disaster than insatiability, no greater wrong than endless desire.

Duke Huan (Qi Huangong, 685-643 B.C.) once asked his advisor Guan Zhong, "Is there a limit to wealth?" Guan Zhong said, "The limit of water is where there is no water, and the limit of wealth is where people stop. But people often do not know what is enough, and this will eventually lead them to their doom. Perhaps this doom represents the limit of wealth."

Seeing the subtle is called illumination. Keeping flexible is called strength.

A pair of sparrows was nesting under the eaves of a house. They had shelter, warmth, and chirped with pride from morning to night.

One day, a seagull came, and, circling overhead, issued a warning: "The chimney of this house is bad! Look how the sparks and embers rise up whenever a fire is lit. It is very dangerous." But the sparrows ignored the seagull's words and went on with their lives. Soon there were eggs in the nest.

Later, the seagull warned them yet again: "Mark my words: There will be a fire soon. Move away before it's too late!"

So comfortable were the sparrows that again they

failed to heed the seagull's warning.

The next time the seagull flew overhead all he saw was the blackened, burned-out patch where the house once stood.

The best tactician does not engage the enemy.

There was once a traveling swordsman skilled in martial arts. One day, he suddenly came the bank of a wide river with no bridge in sight. There on the sandy shore in a small boat was another skilled swordsman practicing his technique. The traveling swordsman boasted of his skill, which made the swordsman in the boat regard him as arrogant and conceited. The traveling swordsman wanted to learn the boat swordsman's style. The boat swordsman calmly said, "I am a master of the 'empty-handed' sword." At this, the traveling swordsman's interest was piqued. "I've never heard of it," he chuckled. The boat swordsman calmly went on, "Once my sword is taken out of its sheath, well...."

"Well what?" demanded the traveling swordsman.

"Let's just say that no other style or technique of *kongfu* can match it."

"Impossible! I challenge you!" said the traveling swordsman.

The boat swordsman smiled wryly and said, looking around, "There's no room here. Let's try the opposite bank."

So the traveling swordsman stepped lightly into the boat while the boat swordsman made for the opposite bank. Just as the boat was about to strike the other shore, the traveling swordsman hopped off lightly, eagerly drawing his sword. Immediately, the boat swordsman checked the boat, and, using his skill as an oarsman, proceeded to turn the boat around and take it back to the bank they had come from. The traveling swordsman stood, incredulous, as the boat swordsman held up his hand.

"*This* is the 'empty-handed' sword!" The boat swordsman exclaimed.

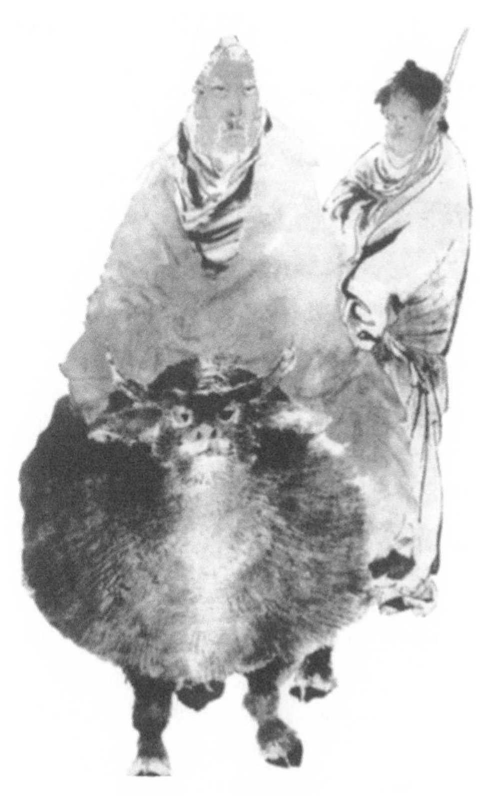

There is nothing better than to know that you don't know. There is nothing worse than not knowing, yet thinking you know.

Cao Han was a general in the Song Dynasty. One day, he came to Yuantong Temple at Mount Lu, where he sought the Buddhist monk, Yuande. Cao Han said, "Master, can you tell me how to gain the courage and wisdom to win in battle?" Yuande replied "I do not know of war." Yuande, wise and learned though he was, was thus not ashamed of not knowing war. Had he given Cao Han bad advice, it would have been worse than not knowing of something at all.

Whereas the force of words is soon spent. Far better is it to keep what is in the heart.

In a small village there was a pretty girl who gossiped endlessly. She talked about this person and that person; soon all her neighbors kept their distance and said not one word to her, lest she gossip about them some more. It was no surprise, then, that when she had reached the age at which most girls get married, she received not one proposal. Crushed, the girl went to ask the highly respected village elder for help. "Though you are quite beautiful," the elder told her, "You also gossip unceasingly about other people. This is not correct behavior. To overcome this, go to the market and buy a chicken, then pluck it as you walk home."

The girl did as she was told, purchasing a chicken at the market and plucking its feathers as she walked home.

"Very good!" said the elder. "Now, you must gather the scattered feathers together. If you can complete this task, everyone will like you."

The girl looked horrified. "But the feathers have long been blown away by wind!"

"Just as the feathers were scattered by the wind," said the elder "Your thoughtless gossiping has spread across the village. Much harm and ill will have you trailed behind you. Can you collect them all back again? Think carefully before you speak!"

The kind is the teacher of the unkind, as he can educate the unkind to be kind; the unkind is the mirror of the kind, as he can warn the kind to degenerate.

At the end of emperor Han Gaozu's rule, Liu Bang ascended the throne. Liu Bang was not devoted to the task of governance. The Confucian scholar Lu Jia called on him to read *The Book of Poetry*, and *The Book of History*. At this, Liu Bang was infuriated and scolded Lu Jia loudly: "I seized the throne from horseback! What possible use is *The Book of Poetry*, and *The Book of History* to me?" Lu Jia spoke bluntly, "Sire, you can seize the state from horseback, but how can you hold on to it from horseback? Both the emperor Tang of the Shang dynasty and the emperor Wu of the Zhou dynasty took power during adverse times and held it during peaceful times. They were adept in the use of the writing brush and the sword, and their reigns were long and stable. If the first emperor of Qin followed the examples of previous emperors to carry out benevolent policies after seizing the regime, then how could the Qin have collapsed?" Liu Bang realized the gravity of Lu Jia's words and from then on, was devoted to the task of governance.

8

Accomplish without boast. Accomplish without arrogance. Accomplish without conceit.

Confucius was once asked about two disciples: "Who is better, Zizhang or Zixia?" Confucius replied: "Zizhang is too much, and Zixia is not enough." In this way, Confucius did not give an answer as to who was better.

"So, which of the two is better?" He was asked.

Confucius instead replied, "Too much is as bad as too little."

The reason the sea can be regarded as the ruler of all the valley streams is because of its lowness. All the other streams flow into it. Thus, its humility gives it power.

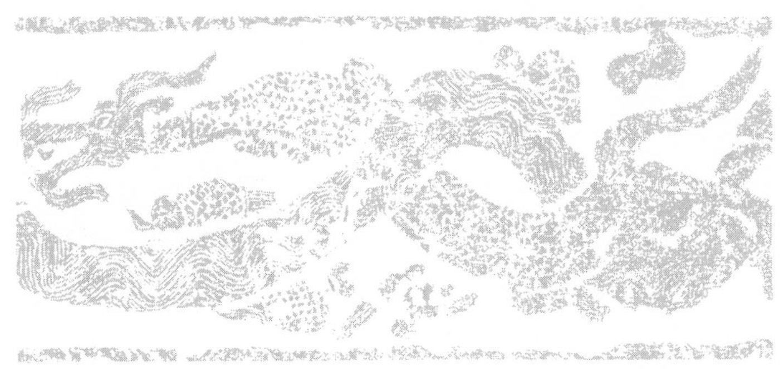

A disappointed young man had been traveling for ten years and at last he came to Fayuan Temple. He said to the abbot, Shiyuan, "I want to learn the art of painting, but I have not found a satisfactory teacher.

Shiyuan asked, "You mean you have traveled north and south for ten years, yet you didn't find a teacher?" The young man sighed, "The reputation of many teachers is undeserved; some are not even as good as I am!" Shiyuan smiled faintly and said, "Since your painting is on par with the famous masters, please paint something for me. Can you draw a teapot and cups for me?

The young man said, "That's too easy!" After a

few strokes, he had painted a teapot and an elegant cup. He asked Shiyuan whether he was satisfied.

Shiyuan said, "Your technique is good, but put the cup and teapot upside down. The teapot should be below and the cup should be above!"

The young man frowned, "The water is poured from the teapot to the cup; how can you put the cup above the teapot?"

Shiyuan gave a wry smile. "So, you know this as the truth. You want to fill your cup with the aroma of those famous masters, yet you put your own cup so high! How can the tea be poured? Only by putting yourself in a position to receive can you absorb the wisdom and experience of others. The young man blushed and suddenly realized that Shiyuan was right. From then on, he was humble and eager to learn. slightly, "So, you know this to be the truth! You want to fill your cup with wisdom and talent of those famous masters like so much tea, yet you put your cup even higher than the teapot; how can the tea be poured into your cup? Only by putting yourself lower than others can you absorb other people's wisdom and experience."

The young man blushed and suddenly realized that Shiyuan was right. From then on, he was humble and eager to learn.

Thus the sage understands of himself, but does not show himself, loves himself but does not prize himself.

In the Tang Dynasty, after Emperor Taizong ascended to the throne, he did not show disdain to his courtiers or to the common people because of his supremacy. He knew well the parable: "Water can support a boat; water can also overturn it." Taizong knew that an emperor's rule lay in the hearts of its people. He said, "The fate of the emperor lay in the hearts of the people; I stabilized the Turks and the Tiele, swept across the desert and obtained the obedience of the Yi and Di, and won a wide reputation stretching even to Korea. But, I am afraid to become extravagant and arrogant; I am always self-examining; I hope that each one of my ministers shall speak bluntly; for I will accept good ideas to govern the country. In this way, we can make our country have stability and longevity.

Also Available

The Art of War

ISBN 1-59265-000-2

A Basic Confucius

ISBN 1-59265-040-8

A Basic Mencius

ISBN 1-59265-046-0